CATHOLIC &

SKILLS FOR SPIRITUAL GROWTH

# HOW TO LIVE A MORAL LIFE

*BY*
*MIKE CAROTTA*

RESOURCES FOR CHRISTIAN LIVING™
Allen, Texas

NIHIL OBSTAT
Rev. Msgr. Glenn D. Gardner, J.C.D.
Censor Librorum

IMPRIMATUR
† Most Rev. Charles V. Grahmann
Bishop of Dallas

April 28, 1997

The Nihil Obstat and Imprimatur are official declarations that the material reviewed is free of doctrinal or moral error. No implication is contained therein that those granting the Nihil Obstat and Imprimatur agree with the contents, opinions, or statements expressed.

BOOK DESIGN: Dennis Davidson

COVER DESIGN: Bob Shema

PHOTO CREDITS

Gary Buss/FPG International 15

Ron Chapple/FPG International 33

B. Daemmrich/The ImageWorks 17

Full Photographics, Inc. 7

Mark Gordon/Index Stock Photography 22T

Robert Hitchman/Unicorn Stock Photos 34

David Honl/Gamma Liaison 35B

Ted Horowitz/The Stock Market 12

Index Stock Photography 25

Uniphoto 22B

Wide World Photos 18

ACKNOWLEDGMENTS

Scripture quotations are from the New Revised Standard Version of the Bible, copyright 1989 by the Division of Christian Education of the National Council of the Churches of Christ in the USA. Used by permission. All rights reserved.

The "Circles of L.I.F.E." activity is adapted from *Sex and the Teenager* by Kieran Sawyer, Copyright © 1990 by Ave Maria Press, Notre Dame, IN. Used by permission. All rights reserved.

"Handle It," "Poet's Page," "Photo Poll," and "Coping with a Friend's or a Parent's Substance Abuse" are materials that first appeared in *Off the Record*, a youth supplement to *The Record*, the weekly diocesan newspaper in the Archdiocese of Louisville. Used with permission.



Send all inquiries to:
RCL • Resources for Christian Living
200 East Bethany Drive
Allen, Texas 75002-3804

Toll free 800–822–6701
Fax 800–688–8356

Printed in the United States of America

**20211** ISBN 0-7829-0733-4

1 2 3 4 5 01 00 99 98 97

# Contents

# VIRTUE-al REALITY

Can virtues be taught? Socrates, Plato, Aristotle, and other early philosophers wondered a lot about this. Today, people are encouraging our society to "return to virtue."

## Do you think a person can learn how to practice virtues?

What are virtues, anyway? Virtues are positive habits and attitudes that allow us to perform good acts. They are acquired by human effort; that is, a person intentionally develops or "practices" the moral virtues in order to live a morally good life.

The Catholic Church points to four moral, or cardinal, virtues, which are found in the Old Testament Book of Wisdom (8:7). They are the four virtues of **prudence**, **justice**, **fortitude**, and **temperance.** These four virtues play a pivotal role in our moral life. They are called "cardinal" virtues because all other human virtues connect to or hinge on them—the word *cardinal* comes from a Latin word meaning "hinge on."

Unlike the word *justice,* the words *prudence, fortitude,* and *temperance* are not real familiar. So try this:

## Prudence

***Prudence*** **refers to sound reasoning—the kind of reasoning that leads to right actions . . . good thinking that leads to good acts . . . wise judgment that leads to decent conduct. Get it?**

## Justice

***Justice*** **is about fairness and the consistent desire to give everyone their rights even when it means you may lose something—like friends, popularity, money, or privilege.**

# Fortitude

***Fortitude*** **is courage to do the right thing and strength to overcome difficulties.**

# Temperance

***Temperance*** **is all about moderation and balance. It is about controlling your impulses and desires within the limits of what's honorable—even when no one is looking or cares.**

The Church also points to three "theological" virtues: **faith**, **hope**, and **charity** (love). These virtues reflect the ways we relate to God. The three theological virtues are the foundation of our life with God and help us live the four moral virtues.

AND NOW FAITH, HOPE, AND LOVE ABIDE, THESE THREE; AND THE GREATEST OF THESE IS LOVE.

1 CORINTHIANS 13:13

So, do you agree with Socrates? Can virtues be taught?

**Catholic & Capable** will introduce you to SKILLS that will help you to practice virtues and live the moral life as a person of conscience, character, and contribution. Thanks for your willingness to work with this program. With God's grace, you can make your own new virtue-al reality.

# RECOGNIZING VIRTUES

*Directions*: Write your answers to these questions as you review the story "Our Daily Bread." Then discuss your answers with the group.

**1.** What do you think Dorothy meant when she described compassion as a balance between passion and principles?

**2.** What do you think is meant by the statement, "When you have the faith of a child, you will always be home"?

**3.** What do you think Janet meant when she said, "We are all Manger People"?

**4.** What do you think was the significance of Eleanor's advice, "Take one step at a time"?

**5.** Why do you think Eleanor took the time to tell Wyatt, "Strength . . . means doing the right thing"?

**6.** Which virtues (prudence, justice, fortitude, temperance, faith, hope, charity) did you recognize in each crew member? Give examples to support your opinions.

God's grace helps us to practice virtues and to live a moral life as a person of conscience, character, and contribution. Think about the kind of life you are leading in school, at home, and in your community. Then take a moment to complete the following statements by circling the response that best describes "you" right now. Briefly explain why you rated yourself as you did.

**1.** Conscience guides me to know right from wrong and encourages me to choose what is good. I demonstrate prudence and I believe I follow my conscience:

**a.** always **b.** most of the time **c.** sometimes **d.** seldom

I chose letter _____ because

**2.** Honesty, integrity, trustworthiness, respect, compassion, and responsibility are signs of true character. I believe I am developing:

**a.** a very strong character **b.** a character that is most often worthy of trust
**c.** a good character that still needs some further development

I chose letter _____ because

**3.** I am learning to tell right from wrong MOSTLY by listening to the wisdom of:

**a.** the Church **b.** the Bible **c.** my family **d.** all three

I chose letter _____ because

**4.** Through my contribution to others, I help to continue Christ's work on earth by practicing the virtue of justice. In my daily life I try to make a difference through acts of service, caring, and compassion:

**a.** frequently **b.** sometimes **c.** once in a while

I chose letter _____ because

**5.** When I think of God's grace and the theological virtues, I would like to grow in the virtue of:

**a.** faith **b.** hope **c.** charity

I chose letter _____ because

# Do Circumstances Make a Difference?

*Directions*: These eight situations are examples of a morally wrong action. For each action, try to add a sentence that makes the action "less wrong."

Be prepared to explain your response.

**1.** You let two friends copy your answers on a test.

**2.** Your parents ask you where you are going tonight and you lie—big-time.

**3.** A person kidnaps a seven-year-old girl and then tortures and kills her.

**4.** Someone sells drugs to a six-year-old, who becomes addicted.

**5.** Several of your friends ridicule someone of a different race.

**6.** Someone takes your sunglasses.

**7.** A classmate deliberately spreads the false rumor that you and the person you are dating are having sex.

**8.** Two seniors on your team get into a fight and break the trophy case in the school hallway. The coach suspends you and the rest of the seniors on the team until the two guilty seniors step forward, which they refuse to do.

YOUR WORD IS A LAMP TO MY FEET
AND A LIGHT TO MY PATH.
I HAVE SWORN AN OATH
AND CONFIRMED IT,
TO OBSERVE YOUR RIGHTEOUS
ORDINANCES.

PSALM 119:105–6

# DISTINGUISHING RIGHT FROM WRONG

Human acts are either good or evil. The Catholic Church teaches that the "rightness" or "wrongness" of an action or behavior depends on three things: the **act**, the **intention**, and the **circumstances.** You need to consider all three of these elements, with one element—the act—being more important than the other two.

Living a moral life involves the ability to tell when some human *acts* are wrong "no matter what." When we believe that some action of ours is wrong—no matter what, we are judging the wrongness of the act regardless of our personal intention or circumstances. This judgment is referred to as *objective* moral reasoning.

Living a moral life involves allowing ourselves to submit to a higher authority than ourselves, namely, God and God's law. While we believe God to be understanding and compassionate, we also believe that God has revealed to us that some behaviors are objectively wrong—wrong no matter what.

The *intention* of the person committing the act is also related to the skill of distinguishing between right and wrong. Go back to the story "Our Daily Bread." Everyone was performing a good act by serving others, yet one of the crew was serving with the intention of having it look good on college applications. Remember? Not the same as the crew member who served with the intention of helping out. Good intentions can really help you tell right from wrong—but don't be fooled by them. Some good intentions can't justify an act that is objectively wrong. Helping a friend is a good intention, but your intention—helping—can't justify buying drugs for that person. (Remember who did that in "Our Daily Bread"?)

The same may be said about the *circumstances* that surround an act. Sometimes the circumstances can help you distinguish right from wrong—for example, taking something that belongs to someone else because you are being forced to. Yet circumstances can't change the wrongful nature of some acts—for example, having sex with someone you aren't married to, because the two of you "love" each other.

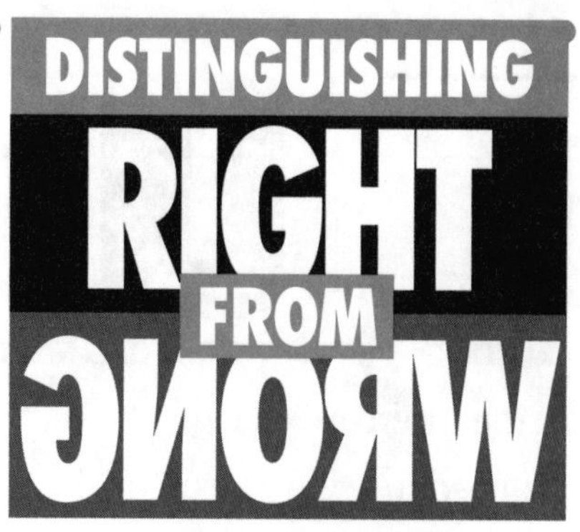


*continued*

When trying to tell the difference between right and wrong, practice examining all three elements—the **act**, the **intention**, and the **circumstances.** These three "sources" of morality will help you, but telling right from wrong is still a tough thing to do. Keep the virtues of prudence, justice, fortitude, temperance, faith, hope, and charity in mind to guide you.

Learning how to tell whether an action is good or evil is at the heart of living a moral life and being a person of conscience.

We all must have a *moral code* that is shaped, in part, by the nonnegotiable teachings of Jesus and the Gospels. We must have a *moral code* that also acknowledges that forgiveness is available to each of us when we admit our morally wrong choices, confess our sins, and seek to reconcile ourselves with those we have wronged.

WHATEVER IS TRUE, WHATEVER IS HONORABLE, WHATEVER IS JUST, WHATEVER IS PURE, WHATEVER IS PLEASING, WHATEVER IS COMMENDABLE, IF THERE IS ANY EXCELLENCE AND IF THERE IS ANYTHING WORTHY OF PRAISE, THINK ABOUT THESE THINGS.

PHILIPPIANS 4:8

# Handle It

1. You are the last person to leave a party. As you rush to your car to be home before curfew, two classmates who have been drinking pull up. After hearing that the party is over, they stumble back into the car, about to drive away.

2. You and everyone else on the team are working hard during off-season practice, conditioning for next year's football season. Four teammates are bulking up with steroids. Two of them will be vying for the same position you've been trying to win for the last three years.

3. A person with a reputation for being sexually active wants to go out with you. You have met this person in class and you like this person as a friend.

4. None of your friends own a car, but you do. Your friends expect you to take them places; however, they never offer to pay for gas.

5. While waiting for class to begin, a classmate of yours describes some serious problems, begins to cry, and briefly mentions thoughts of "saying good-bye" to everyone.

6. A friend's mother has some personal problems and your friend keeps pressuring you for help. You don't want to alienate your friend, but you don't know what to do.

7. You've been helping a lady in your neighborhood pack because she is moving. She promised you five dollars an hour and you've worked ten hours. She pays you only thirty dollars.

# PAYING ATTENTION

After watching the video segment on social issues, practice Analyzing Society's Values and Issues through the process of "paying attention." Then select a topic—such as capital punishment, illegal immigration, abortion, rating TV shows, teen curfew laws, handgun control—and practice applying the process of "paying attention" to the topic you selected.

The process of "paying attention," which helps us practice the skill of Analyzing Society's Values and Issues, involves three consecutive steps: See, Judge, Act.

SEE → JUDGE → ACT

**SEE:** In order to *see* all sides of a social issue, you must notice how people in your school or neighborhood are dealing with the issue. You must also stay current with national news related to the issue. You must be aware of the teachings of the Church and be able to see issues with eyes of faith, and relate them to the values taught by Jesus. If you limit your knowledge of an issue to only those things that directly affect you every day, you will not fully develop the skill of Analyzing Society's Values and Issues.

**JUDGE:** Don't judge an issue without knowing the *facts!* In order to get facts, you need to investigate—to ask questions of friends, family, teachers, and others, and to gather information about the people who are key participants in the situation or suffer from it. You need to reflect on such questions as, What do the Ten Commandments say? What does Scripture say? What does the Church teach about the issue?

Regarding capital punishment, the Church teaches:

> Public authority must redress the violation of personal and social rights by imposing on the offender an adequate punishment for the crime, as a condition for the offender to regain the exercise of his or her freedom. In this way authority also fulfills the purpose of defending public order and ensuring people's safety, while at the same time offering the offender an incentive and help to change his or her behaviour and be rehabilitated. (Cf. *ibid.*)
>
> Pope John Paul II,
> *The Gospel of Life,*
> March 25, 1995 (56)

You have to do your homework before you can judge an issue. If you don't, you'll be acting out of ignorance and look like a fool. And you'll treat others unfairly. But remember, *you have to make a judgment*. If you don't, you are copping out. Don't judge people. God expects you to judge the morality, the rightness or wrongness, of the situation or issue. So the key is this: Make an *informed* judgment. Ask a question. Then ask another one. Get an answer. Then get another one—until you have the facts.

**ACT:** Do something—little thing, big thing, one-time thing, regular thing. But do something. Make a call. Write a letter. Apologize. Give a hug. Send flowers. Spend time with . . . Speak out against . . . Stand up for . . . Go out of your way to . . . After you see and judge, *do something.*

# SEEing TV Shows

*Directions:* This exercise will help you critique society's values and issues by using the "see" step in the process of "paying attention." Watch a TV show and check the appropriate box next to each item on the checklist below. (Check N/A if an item was not portrayed at all on the show.)

**Name of Program**________________________________________

**Date**__________________________**Network**____________________

| | Yes | No | N/A |
|---|---|---|---|
| 1. Does the program give a positive view of minority groups? | ❑ | ❑ | ❑ |
| 2. Is the program free of age stereotypes? For example, does it portray men and women only in traditional roles, young people as irresponsible, children as rebellious, or elderly people as forgetful? | ❑ | ❑ | ❑ |
| 3. Does the program separate fact from fantasy? | ❑ | ❑ | ❑ |
| 4. Does the program promote nonviolent conflict-resolution skills? | ❑ | ❑ | ❑ |
| 5. Does the program reflect gospel values? | ❑ | ❑ | ❑ |
| 6. Are positive things given the same importance as negative or violent ones? | ❑ | ❑ | ❑ |
| 7. Are the attributes and qualities attributed to women limited to beauty? | ❑ | ❑ | ❑ |
| 8. Are women shown at jobs other than those that merely support men? | ❑ | ❑ | ❑ |
| 9. Are fathers shown raising or spending time with children? | ❑ | ❑ | ❑ |
| 10. Do male and female characters respect each other? | ❑ | ❑ | ❑ |
| 11. Are virtues such as trustworthiness, honesty, respect, responsibility, and fairness treated as valuable? | ❑ | ❑ | ❑ |
| 12. Is affection demonstrated appropriately? | ❑ | ❑ | ❑ |

# Poet's Page

## The Bag Lady

by Jamie Beakes, 16

A pale, pale shaft of moonlight
filters through the dark,
hov'ring for a moment's time
beneath a freeway arc.

Huddled near a pillar,
by a quickly dwindling flame,
there lies an ancient woman
shiv'ring against the rain.

Her swarthy skin's like leather;
her silver hair is fine.
Her face, alert yet weary,
is spoilt by signs of time.

The broad hands, worn and
weathered,
clutch tight a massive sack,
which holds a life's possessions
to load upon her back.

This burden great and heavy
is not worldly, though, I fear.
It's oppression and sad memories
of days she held so dear.

Now days are full of sorrow
with love and care from no one.
Her only friends the pigeons,
for together they are shunned.

The worry and depression
shall surely build inside.
The begging and starvation
will surely smother pride.

Yet, still, each day she rises
with her load upon her back
to face the new day's waiting
gloom
and walk life's lonely track.

## He Pleaded Insanity

by Barbara Hilton, 16

It causes him to laugh out loud
for no reason at all.
It gives him thoughts of torture,
too intense for others to imagine.
It causes him to be full of unprovoked rage,
enough to kill.
It makes him cautious of getting too close,
because the secret cannot be revealed.

Eyes covered with red veins,
like a confusing road map.
Hair coiled and out of place,
like broken springs of an ancient mattress.
An uneasy grin,
as if he is a tiger ready to pounce.

Always scheming and plotting,
for sure it is his destiny.
He has no options;
he has no peace.

## Roaming

by Mat Herron, 17

Here, now,
we hand ourselves
over to another day of
endless frustrations and
whatever is left of everything.
We give ourselves to the street.
My friend
you know I'm unfaithful in practice
a great judge of
everyone else's character . . .
except my own.
And each feeling that stumbles
across your heart,
is felt in mine as well.
In the numerous times that you have fought me
wrought me,
they give me
one more reassurance
that you don't mean the things you say.
We have this life
one road
the sun blow-torched on our faces
and time.
Can we call it forever?

## The Morning After

by Melody Thurman, 17

The waves lapping upon
the shore—
The sunrise glistening over
each wave—
A terrible pain rips through
my head.
Oh, my brain, will it explode?
What happened last night?
Where was I now?

Think. Think. Think.
A party—
The blaring music—
Some drinks—
Those guys—
My head pounding—
Friends went off—
More drinks—
More guys—
It was wild.
It was fun at first,
But then,
NO!

The "walk" on the beach—
The violating—
The commands—
So rough—
So cruel—
Screams through my head—
I was all alone with these
animals.

Where were my friends?

Where had they gone?
Why had they left me?
Where was I now?
What had they done?

The questions—
The pain—
The fear—
I am all alone.

My mother—
My father—
I longed to go home—
Away from this beach—
Away from this pain.

They stole from me
What I can not get back.
Ripped from my heart
What was precious,
That I was withholding
For that someone I will love.

Stripped of my rights—
My dignity—
And my confidence.

I lie here on this deserted
beach.
Me,
My pain,
And the morning after.

Students are still writing racist comments in their yearbook quotes. There are still bus fights between black students and white students. Not only does racism still exist, but it's prevalent in the citizens of this country not even born when Martin Luther King, Jr. made his famous speech in Washington, D.C.

It's not a black thing. Not a white thing. Not a Hispanic thing, or a Chinese thing. It's a hate thing.

Racism isn't so much using derogatory terms or physically attacking someone because of the way he or she looks. It isn't the fear of another riot that keeps students awake at night and distracted in class. Any student can tell you it doesn't take that much.

"People say racist things like, 'All you black people do this,'" says Vic Bryant, an African American and a junior. "Black people do it, too. They might say, 'White people aren't as good at sports as blacks.'"

Jamie Melendez will assure you that it isn't just a black/white issue anymore. An immigrant from El Salvador, she came to the U.S. knowing very little English, which hindered her abilities to stand up for herself. Jamie now speaks more fluent English than a good number of natives. This, coupled with a few years for her peers to grow up and a change to the Catholic school system, has made racism more of a memory from her youth than a current reality. She can recall kids talking about "'All you Hispanics . . .' and sometimes it was just me, or not me at all," Jamie says.

Aaron Wallace, a Caucasian senior, sees racism all over his school. "I see all kinds of racism. I see a white kid talk bad about a black kid. A black kid talks bad about a white kid. Even black kids talk bad about another black kid, or white kids talk about white kids. Most everybody, in one way or another, is racist. It's endless," he says.

So it is comments that bother students the most, but it isn't comments that appear on the cover of the newspaper and on the six o'clock newscast. It's the events, the fights. It can give students a bad reputation, but as Vic says, "There are certain people who try to get everyone riled up." Vic can tell that these people are usually pinned with a reputation among students.

Racism affects students' performances. Comments take their toll on students, including Aaron, who simplified the problem: "If you can't concentrate 100 percent on what you're studying, you'll have trouble learning."

Racism is a problem. No amendment to the Constitution can make it disappear, and it seems that thirty years of equality may have only amounted to equal racism. Racism isn't going to go away because of someone's speech, and probably not because of one article, either. What miracle could make it disappear?

"All the students need to open their minds," Aaron says. "If you're closed-minded under any circumstances, you're going to be hateful. That's what racism is."

# Not All Violence Is Bloody

The Catholic bishops of the United States have written about violence. Read and reflect on this teaching.

Not all violence is deadly. It begins with anger, intolerance, impatience, unfair judgments, and aggression. It is reflected in our language, our entertainment, our driving, our competitive behavior, and the way we treat our environment. These acts and attitudes are not the same as abusive behavior or physical attacks, but they create a climate where violence prospers and peace suffers. . . . Less obvious and less visible is the slow motion violence of discrimination and poverty, hunger and hopelessness, addiction and self-destructive behavior. This growing culture of violence reflected in some aspects of our public life and entertainment media must be confronted. But it is not just our policies and programming that must change; it is our hearts. And the glorification of violence in movies and music.

*Confronting a Culture of Violence: A Catholic Framework for Action* (USCC, 1996)

# Different Forms of Violence

**Violence takes different forms: *physical, emotional, spiritual.* Each form of violence can be committed either by *individuals* or by *groups.***

**1.** Give an example of physical violence.

**2.** What is the difference between emotional violence and spiritual violence?

**3.** How often have you seen violence in the last six months?

**4.** When was the last time you were actually involved in violence?

# Different Forms of Violence *continued*

**5.** Name the first two MOST violent movies, songs, TV shows, or books that come to your mind.

a.

b.

**6.** Give two examples of nonphysical violence.

a.

b.

**7.** Give one example of nonphysical violence you saw in school recently.

**8.** Use a symbol or an initial to indicate a time when you have inflicted nonphysical violence on someone recently.

# Dealing with Violence

The Gospels give this account of the arrest of Jesus. Describe the role that violence played in Jesus' arrest.

Immediately, while [Jesus] was still speaking, Judas, one of the twelve, arrived; and with him there was a crowd with swords and clubs, from the chief priests, the scribes, and the elders. Now the betrayer had given them a sign, saying, "The one I will kiss is the man; arrest him and lead him away under guard." So when he came, he went up to him at once and said, "Rabbi!" and kissed him. Then they laid hands on him and arrested him. But one of those who stood near drew his sword and struck the slave of the high priest, cutting off his ear. Then Jesus said to them, "Have you come out with swords and clubs to arrest me as though I were a bandit? Day after day I was with you in the temple teaching, and you did not arrest me. But let the scriptures be fulfilled." All of them deserted him and fled.

A certain young man was following him, wearing nothing but a linen cloth. They caught hold of him, but he left the linen cloth and ran off naked.

Mark 14:43–52

## There are four basic ways to respond to violence:

FIGHT BACK.

FLEE.

ACCEPT IT.

NONVIOLENTLY CONFRONT IT.

## Which of these four responses can you find in the story of Jesus' arrest?

Of the following examples of emotional violence, which do you think are worth confronting? Why?

Prejudice

Put-downs

Sexual pressure

Gossip

Intimidation

Exploitation of friends

# NONVIOLENTLY CONFRONT...

1. You are with some friends at the mall. A couple of your friends start telling racist jokes. You don't feel comfortable with their jokes, but everyone else is laughing.

2. You are taking a test for a major grade in algebra class. You notice that your friend sitting next to you has been copying from your paper.

3. Every week on the night before trash day, someone rides by and knocks over every trash can on your block. The people in the neighborhood are trying to catch the person or group who is doing this, but no one can. One night you see your brother and his friends knocking over the trash cans.

4. Your server has just given you and your friends the check for your meals. You all realize that, together, you are a "buck" short. Someone points out that there is a four-dollar tip on the table next to yours.

5. A classmate is coming to school with bruises from "working around the house." You know that this is domestic abuse.

6. Good friends of yours talk filthy. You hate it.

7. Late in a game, your team is down by a bunch. Some members of the other team are talking trash big-time. One of them makes a derogatory comment about your parents.

8. Some kids at school are always "bragging" about their sexual experiences, leaving you out of the conversation. After your latest date with a nice person, they now press you to tell them "all the details."

## In their teachings about violence, the Catholic bishops of the United States have this to say:

Fundamentally, our society needs a moral revolution to replace a culture of violence. . . . God's wisdom, love and commandments can show us the way to live, heal and reconcile. "Thou shalt not kill; Thou shalt not steal" are more than words to be recited. . . . Our faith challenges each of us to an ethic that cherishes life, puts people before things, and values kindness and compassion over anger and vengeance.

Perhaps the greatest challenge is the call for all of us to examine our own lives, to identify how we can choose generosity over selfishness. . . . In many small ways, each of us can help overcome violence by dealing with it on our block. . . . Violence is overcome day by day, choice by choice, person by person. All of us must make a contribution.

*Confronting a Culture of Violence: A Catholic Framework for Action* (USCC, 1996)

# CAN I GET A DO-OVER?

*Directions:* Create a symbol or write an initial or a word that represents a situation in which you would like a second chance. Make sure it is a current situation.

# Don't Make It Worse

*Directions:* Pick four situations below. For each situation you select,

- come up with an excuse that someone might make.
- describe what that person should do in order to keep that first mistake from becoming two mistakes.

1. **Paul** took money from his mom's purse without asking.
2. **Juanita** is looking at another student's answers during a test.
3. **Barry** scratched his initials on the top of his desk and was given detention.
4. **Lee** stayed home from school because he hadn't finished an assignment.
5. **Marrissa** called her mom a very nasty name and was grounded for a month.
6. **Phan** was caught smoking in school.
7. **Phil** punched someone and may be suspended from school.
8. **Merritt** ate nine cookies, and there are only three left for the rest of the family.
9. **Sarasita** is already one hour past her curfew.
10. **Carlos** illegally purchased alcohol.
11. **LaTona** is already ten minutes late for school.
12. **Bree** told a nasty customer to stop bossing her around.
13. **Sergio** has just told his boss, "You're not very smart."
14. **Rachel** lost her money for lunch for the week.
15. **Bob** called a 900 number three times last week from home.
16. **Mandy** left her locker open, and everything in it was taken.
17. **Carole** lost the key to her house.
18. **Ethan** lied to his teacher about understanding the math that was being taught.
19. **Miranda** went to a party even though she knew drugs would be available there.
20. **Missy** hit a mailbox on the side of the road with her car.

# SECOND CHANCES

You can't always get a second chance: you get cut from the team, fail for the semester, get pregnant, wreck the family car, experience the death of a loved one, move to another state, and so on. But most of the time you can get a second chance. You get the chance to make up for a mistake—like those listed on the previous page.

Here is a four-step process that will help you develop the skill of obtaining second chances.

Learn the four steps by associating them with the letters INRI. Follow the steps if you want better performance in some area of your life in which you desire a second chance—like improving a low grade, spending your money more wisely, getting the right summer job, or paying better attention to the people you associate with.

If the second chance directly involves another person, learn how to verbalize the four steps of INRI concretely. For example:

**I:** "____________ (Person's name),

I know I ____________ (Identify your mistake)."

**N:** (Pause—with no excuses.)

**R:** "I will ____________ (Responsible action must follow)."

**I:** "It is really important to me that

____________ (Identify your goal)."

Practice the skill of obtaining second chances by applying the four steps to the situations listed on the previous page. For example:

Pretend you are Missy (last situation) and you hit a mailbox with your car. You could say, "Mom, Dad, I know I hit the mailbox and wasn't as careful as I should have been. I won't make any excuses. I'll have the mailbox fixed, and from now on I'll watch where I'm going. It's really important to me that I drive well."

# WALK ON WATER

*Directions:* Read and reflect on this gospel story. Describe what lesson the gospel story teaches about reaching your goals—especially when the weather in your life is stormy.

Immediately [Jesus] made the disciples get into the boat and go on ahead to the other side, while he dismissed the crowds. And after he had dismissed the crowds, he went up the mountain by himself to pray. When evening came, he was there alone, but by this time the boat, battered by the waves, was far from the land, for the wind was against them. And early in the morning he came walking toward them on the sea. But when the disciples saw him walking on the sea, they were terrified, saying, "It is a ghost!" And they cried out in fear. But immediately Jesus spoke to them and said, "Take heart, it is I; do not be afraid."

Peter answered him, "Lord, if it is you, command me to come to you on the water." He said, "Come." So Peter got out of the boat, started walking on the water, and came toward Jesus. But when he noticed the strong wind, he became frightened, and beginning to sink, he cried out, "Lord, save me!"

MATTHEW 14:22–30

# To Tell the Truth . . .

Think about ways you would practice truth telling in each of these situations.

**1.** You pull out of the parking lot after the movies and accidentally clip another car. Even though the damage is noticeable, your friend says, "Don't worry about it. I've done it before, too. Just go."

**2.** You discover that your eighth-grade brother or sister drank wine coolers last Friday after school. Not for the first time. Your parents don't know.

**3.** Your best friend since grade school has been spreading a false rumor that eventually gets someone suspended.

**4.** A great teacher for whom you have a lot of respect is getting scammed by a student. Everyone knows it—except the teacher.

**5.** A classmate comes to you with someone else's assignment in hand—and a mischievous grin, saying, "Put this under your desk and forget about it." You feel suspicious about it.

**6.** A close friend gets a job as an assistant manager of a record store. You bring three CDs to the counter, trying to decide which two to purchase. Your friend says, "Take all three. I'll just charge you for two. The inventory system is so bad here that they never know what they have. Even my manager takes stuff home."

**7.** Your school store allows students to buy computer software at a 38 percent discount, provided they sign a written certification that it is for personal use only. A good friend needs the software but cannot afford to pay the discounted price of $295. Your friend wants to make a copy of your software, saying, "Everybody buys software for friends and relatives, and the school knows it."

# Truth-Telling Proverbs

There are six things that the Lord hates,
seven that are an abomination to God:
Haughty eyes,
a lying tongue,
and hands that shed innocent blood,
a heart that devises wicked plans,
feet that hurry to run to evil,
a lying witness who testifies falsely,
and one who sows discord in a family.

PROVERBS 6:16–19 (slightly adapted)

Fine speech is not becoming to a fool;
still less is false speech to a ruler.

PROVERBS 17:7

The getting of treasures by a lying tongue
is a fleeting vapor and a snare of death.

PROVERBS 21:6

Truthful lips endure forever,
but a lying tongue lasts only a moment.
Deceit is in the mind of those who plan evil,
but those who counsel peace have joy.
No harm happens to the righteous,
but the wicked are filled with trouble.
Lying lips are an abomination to the Lord,
but those who act faithfully are his delight.

PROVERBS 12:19–22

A lying tongue hates its victims,
and a flattering mouth works ruin.

PROVERBS 26:28

Write your own truth-telling proverbs right here.

# PHOTO POLL

## Who or what has helped form your conscience?

When my parents were divorced when I was five, I started thinking it was my fault. From that point on I kept thinking about whether it was right or wrong. I guess you could say that's how I first began to form my conscience.

KARINA CALIZ, 16

## What does it take to tell the truth?

To tell the truth, sometimes it takes conviction. But I prefer to tell the truth rather than deal with the painful consequences of dishonesty.

STEVE ADAMS, 17

## How many of your friends support dating and waiting?

As far as I know, my entire circle of friends has made a decision to choose abstinence. It's especially important to choose a boyfriend/ girlfriend who can back you up on this. I found the best way to remain strong and comfortable with your decision is to talk openly about it with your friends and significant other and most importantly pray to God and the Virgin Mary for strength.

JAMIE BEAKES, 17

What my parents have taught me and seeing how my positive role models act.

MARIFE BAUTISTA, 18

I think that ultimately I developed a moral conscience on my own with help from God. Yet I think my parents and teacher have influenced my moral conscience the most.

CLAIRE MUGAVIN, 17

Telling the truth takes strength and intelligence. Strength to have the guts to handle any consequences that may follow, and intelligence to know it is the best way to handle any situation.

JULIE JANES, 17

To tell the truth, I think it takes a strong will and praying—especially when lying would be easier.

JENNIFER STOBER, 18

All of 'em. We don't want to take a chance of losing out on our high school and young adult years—and we really respect the people we date.

DAN DENTINGER, 17

In the public school I go to, the numbers are very low. Most of my close friends support it, but we never even talk about the subject much.

JASON JAGGERS, 16

# Circles of L.I.F.E.

We can experience God's love through our relationships with other people, because God is "in each of us." Moral living is all about treating people lovingly. Knowing the difference between the various relationships of love, infatuation, friendship, and exploitation helps us to be fair, honest, sincere, and true to ourselves. Ask yourself:

**How have I experienced infatuation? Friendship? Love? Exploitation?**

These different relationships share common characteristics. Sometimes love and infatuation can look the same. Friendship and love have a lot in common; so do infatuation and friendship. If you look closely, you can see that infatuation also shares some common characteristics with exploitation, and that exploitation shares some common characteristics with friendship. However, there is never any real connection between love and exploitation. Love and exploitation will always be completely separate and opposite.

A. ______________________

B. ______________________

C. ______________________

D. ______________________

E. ______________________

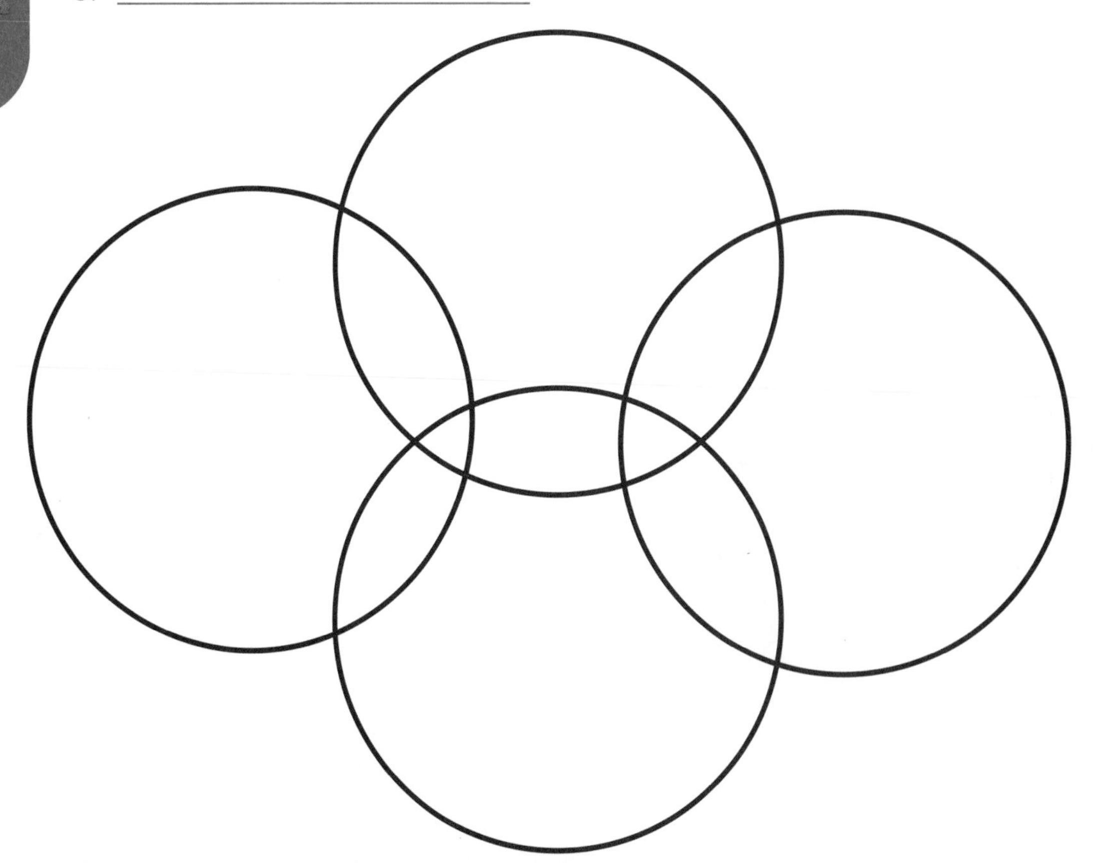

# Building and Maintaining Relationships

Moral living involves being a person of **conscience, character,** and **contribution.** Your moral life comes together in the way you care for others, not only those people you have known for a long time, but also those that God brings into your life for a short time.

In a complex and stressful world, all of us can pay attention to the way we *contribute* to the rest of God's family. We can *contribute* to society, to our community, our school, and our family in a "zillion" ways. Jesus gave us some examples of how to "pay attention" to others: Feed the hungry. Shelter the homeless. Clothe the naked. Visit the sick. Love one another.

Here are some suggestions that will help you deliberately *contribute* in your everyday way of caring for others.

**Initiate contact:** Do not wait for someone else to start. Take a risk. Reach out. Knock on the door. Show up. Make the call. Write the letter. E-mail someone.

**Acquaint yourself with someone else's passion:** Find out what "fuels" someone's life. Discover what captures their dreams and interests, deep down and below the surface.

**Actively listen:** Work hard at hearing—paying attention to—what someone is actually saying. Don't think about what you want to say in return. Ask the other person to tell you more. Repeat what you think you are hearing. *Contribute* by demonstrating how much you care about others through the effort you make in listening.

**Communicate clearly:** Keep it simple. Use the right words. Do not assume the other person understands what you are getting at—say it straight up. Sometimes it takes concentration. Sometimes it takes courage. (Courage is a virtue, remember?)

**Be empathetic:** This is one of the single most important traits of moral living. Choose someone else's shoes and step inside them. Put yourself aside for a moment and do what it takes to understand what the other person is feeling, thinking, and going through. You do not have to agree or approve—but can you understand?

**Tell the truth:** Honesty and integrity, courage and conscience—these are more valuable than dishonest loyalty. In a world of so much hypocrisy and deception, other people will respect you as a person of character when you practice truth telling.

So then, putting away falsehood, let all of us speak the truth to our neighbors, for we are members of one another. Be angry but do not sin; do not let the sun go down on your anger, and do not make room for the devil. Thieves must give up stealing; rather let them labor and work honestly with their own hands, so as to have something to share with the needy. Let no evil talk come out of your mouths, but only what is useful for building up, as there is need, so that your words may give grace to those who hear. And do not grieve the Holy Spirit of God, with which you were marked with a seal for the day of redemption. Put away from you all bitterness and wrath and anger and wrangling and slander, together with all malice, and be kind to one another, tenderhearted, forgiving one another, as God in Christ has forgiven you.

Ephesians 4:25–32

# The Question of Friendship

Reading and thinking about these questions will help you determine whether you are in a relationship of exploitation and infatuation instead of true friendship and love. You have a right to ask these questions. Unless you ask these questions, you run the risk of being a victim of a relationship and not allowing the relationship to help you live a moral life. Asking these questions will help you be the kind of person you were created to be.

**1.** Can I achieve my goals and still have this relationship?

**2.** How much of my happiness depends on you?

**3.** Can we be people of character?

**4.** How much energy do I spend worrying about being the way you want me to be?

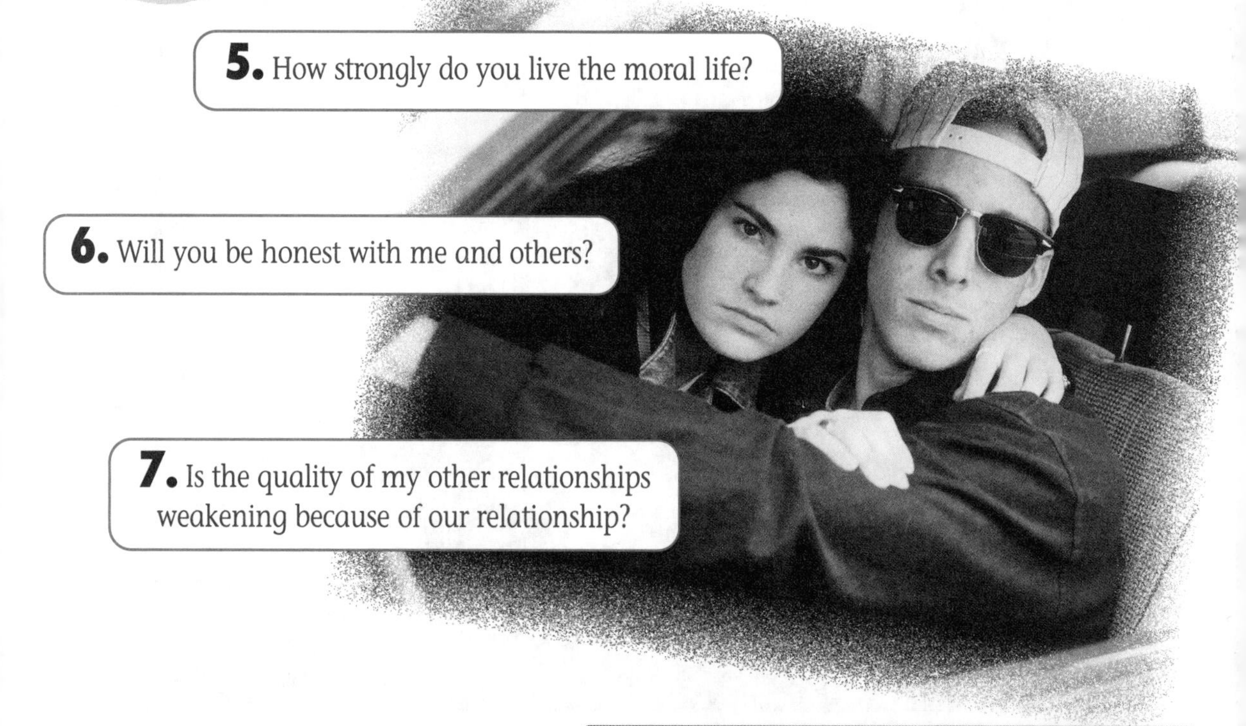

**5.** How strongly do you live the moral life?

**6.** Will you be honest with me and others?

**7.** Is the quality of my other relationships weakening because of our relationship?

# Coping with a Friend's or a Parent's Substance Abuse

BY CINDY CHRISTENSEN,

Ask yourself these questions:

- ***Does someone I care about drink too much?***
- ***Do I worry about a friend's or a parent's drinking or using?***
- ***Do I feel afraid when this person gets angry with me?***
- ***Have I ever lied about a friend's or a parent's drinking or using?***
- ***Have I ever been afraid of riding in a car with someone who has been drinking or using?***
- ***Do I feel guilty about a friend's or a parent's drinking or using?***
- ***Have I ever been embarrassed by a friend's or a parent's behavior when that person has been drinking or using?***
- ***Am I uncomfortable even thinking about these questions?***

If you have answered yes to some of these questions, you are not alone. Four to six students in every classroom are affected by a relationship with someone who has a drinking or using problem. Recognizing that

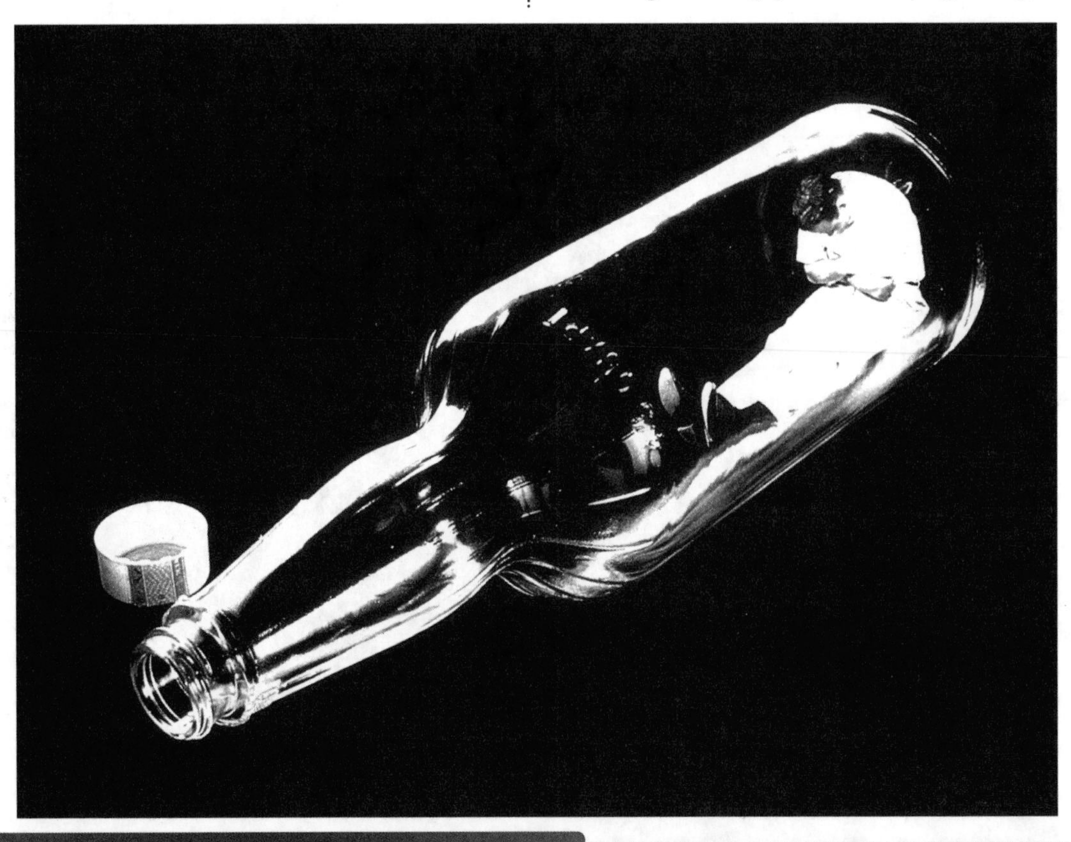

September 21, 1996 Metropo...

## Drunk Driver Kills 16-Year-Old

BOSTON— A drunk driver hit and killed a 16-year-old Boston High School girl yesterday in front of her own home. Doctors worked non-stop for 14 hours trying to revive her but her injuries were determined to be too severe. The drunk driver is in custody and is being held without bond until he can

someone has a problem with alcohol or drugs is the first big step. Trying to *contribute* to that person's recovery is a huge challenge.

Talk confidentially to a counselor or any adult whom you really trust about your concerns and fears. See if there is a support group of other students who are also trying to contribute to someone in the same situation. Try writing down some of your thoughts, feelings, and questions right after something upsetting takes place in that relationship.

What if your friend or your parent has gone way beyond occasional drinking and gets drunk or high every weekend? Can you find a way to let the person know of your concern without yelling or preaching? Can you express your concern without getting fooled into thinking it's no big deal, or that you should understand what the person is going through instead of trying to confront her or him?

Be a good listener. But also be a clear communicator. Speak the truth as you see it. Invite the person to activities that don't require drinking or drugs.

This is tough. Care deeply, but don't get exploited. Believe you can help, but don't believe you can make someone change. Remember that you cannot make someone change. It's not about how good you are at helping people. It's not about how much time you invest in helping someone with an alcohol problem. The person with the drinking or using problem is the only person who can make the change. That's where you have to protect yourself. If alcohol or drugs are making someone a victim, don't let the problem make a victim out of you. Build a certain kind of shield around yourself so that if the person you are worried about and trying to help doesn't make changes, you can still stay focused on your goals, your values, and your potential to be your own person of conscience, character, and contribution.

# Dating and Waiting

View the video segment on "Dating and Waiting" and write an extended essay describing:

- the difficulties of dating and waiting until marriage,
- specific ways to handle sexual pressure, and
- the benefits of choosing chastity as a lifestyle.

# Standing Up for the Moral Life

## PART ONE

**Symbol-bearer One:** (Hold a Bible high and place it reverently on a table in front of the group.)

**Reader One:** Conscience . . . (pause) . . . Because God loves us completely, we are given the freedom to make decisions that will shape our lives and the lives of those around us.

God knows the great responsibility that comes with this freedom. So God has given each of us a conscience to guide us in choosing what is truly right, what it truly good for us and for others.

Forming our conscience means that we learn how to distinguish what is right and what is wrong. Following our conscience means that we think about the consequences of our decisions and how others are affected by those decisions. No one can take the great gift of our conscience away from us; no one can take the awesome responsibility of forming and following our conscience from us.

But God expects us—all of us—to be people of conscience.

How willing are we to include God's law, the Bible, the commandments, the Church, and our parents in the formation of our conscience?

How willing are we to really see, judge, and act?

How willing are we to pay attention?

(Pause)

Conscience.

**Group:** (Feel free to stand at this point if you want to symbolize your willingness to "stand up" for your moral conscience. Remain standing until after the next reading.)

**Reader One:** A reading from the prophet Micah:

> What does the Lord ask of you?
> This and only this:
> that you act justly,
> love tenderly,
> and walk humbly with your God.
> BASED ON MICAH 6:8

## PART TWO

**Symbol-bearer Two:** (Hold a lighted candle high and place it in a stand in front of the group.)

**Reader Two:** Character . . . (pause) . . . Each of us is building our character by the decisions we make, by the virtues we live by, and by the values we hold.

Each of us can choose to tell the truth or lie, be trustworthy or dishonest, treat others fairly or unjustly, show respect toward ourselves and others or be careless and hurtful.

Each of us reveals our character by our relationships and by the way we respond to the many situations we face each day. When we regularly choose to do what is honest, just, courageous, or prudent, when we lead a virtuous life, we reveal our character.

(Pause)

Character.

**Group:** (Feel free to stand at this point if you want to symbolize your willingness to "stand up" for being a person of character. Remain standing until after the next reading.)

**Reader Two:** A reading from the prophet Micah:

> What does the Lord ask of you?
> This and only this:
> that you act justly,
> love tenderly,
> and walk humbly with your God.
> BASED ON MICAH 6:8

## PART THREE

**Symbol-bearer Three:** (Hold a bowl of water and a towel high and place them on a table in front of the group.)

**Reader Three:** Contribution . . . (pause) . . . Jesus told us that in the final judgment we will be judged by the standard of how often we have helped others.

We can make a contribution to better the society in which we live by using our gifts and talents to help those around us, especially those in need.

We are called to serve somebody.
Serve somebody.
Serve somebody.

We can also contribute by the ways we build and maintain relationships with those we encounter every day.

We can build our friendships,
cherish our loved ones,
recognize our infatuations,
and confront exploitation.

(Pause)

Contribution.

**Group:** (Feel free to stand at this point if you want to symbolize your willingness to "stand up" for being a person committed to making a contribution. Remain standing until after the next reading.)

**Reader Three:** A reading from the prophet Micah:

> What does the Lord ask of you?
> This and only this:
> that you act justly,
> love tenderly,
> and walk humbly with your God.
>
> BASED ON MICAH 6:8